Christine Caine & Lisa Harper

The Marvel and Miracle of Advent

Recapturing the Wonder of Jesus Living With Us

 HarperChristian Resources

The Marvel and Miracle of Advent Bible Study Guide
© 2024 by Christine Caine and Lisa Harper

Published in Grand Rapids, Michigan, by HarperChristian Resources. HarperChristian
Resources is a registered trademark of HarperCollins Christian Publishing, Inc.

Requests for information should be sent to customercare@harpercollins.com.

ISBN 978–0–310– 16285-8 (softcover)
ISBN 978–0–310-16286-5 (ebook)

HarperChristian Resources titles may be purchased in bulk for church, business, fundraising, or ministry use. For
information, please e–mail ResourceSpecialist@ChurchSource.com.

Lisa Harper is represented by Alive Literary Agency, www.aliveliterary.com.
Christine Caine is published in association with Yates & Yates, www.yates2.com.

First Printing July 2024 / Printed in the United States of America

Contents

Welcome

From Christine and Lisa

For more than a thousand years, a special time has been set apart in the church calendar that invites us to pause, to prepare, and to anticipate the arrival of the long-awaited Messiah. This season of Advent gives us the time and opportunity to prayerfully reflect on the wonder of Christ's glorious entrance into this world.

I (Chris) was raised in Australia and grew up in the Greek Orthodox Church. For us, December was the kickoff of summer. I heard stories and watched movies of people enjoying white, snowy Christmases; meanwhile, we were enjoying the white sands of the beach. My mom celebrated Advent by preparing different foods, and I'd anxiously count down the days to Christmas with an Advent calendar loaded with chocolate.

Because I (Lisa) spent my childhood in central Florida, I was used to warm winters. However, after relocating to Tennessee, I quickly fell in love with a snowy holiday season accompanied by crackling fires and hot cocoa the way Nat King Cole used to croon about. But while Australia and Florida's weather is relatively similar, Chris and I had very different pre-Christmas experiences, because my sweet, Jesus-loving mom didn't associate Advent with being Protestant. Therefore, it took me a long time to understand that Advent is for everybody, y'all!

Yet what we've both discovered is that, more than just a countdown to Jesus' birthday, this is a season to reflect on Jesus' miraculous birth and the anticipation of His return.

And it's a call to attentiveness, an opportunity to prepare the way for the Lord, that begins in our own hearts. It's a time when the air is thick with the expectation of the dawn of a new day—and we all need that!

As we embark on this journey of Advent together, may you find your hope renewed through the promise of Emmanuel, "God with us." And may you rediscover the love of Christ being born anew in your heart.

Chris Lisa

How to Use This Guide

OVERVIEW

The Marvel and Miracle of Advent Bible study is divided into four sessions. Every session includes Video Notes, Group Discussion, Call to Action, Closing Prayer, and between sessions Personal Study. As a group, you will watch the video and then use the video notes and discussion questions to engage in active conversation. The goal is to develop genuine relationships and to become fully equipped to share the good news of God's love and why His condescension from heaven to be with us matters so very much—not just to cover all the material.

GROUP SIZE

This four-session video Bible study is designed to be experienced in a group setting, such as a Bible study, Sunday school class, retreat, small-group, or online gathering. If your gathering is large, you may want to consider splitting everyone into smaller groups of five to eight people after viewing the teaching for more intimate discussion. This will ensure that everyone has an opportunity to participate in the discussions.

MATERIALS NEEDED

Everyone in your group will need a copy of this study guide, which includes personal streaming video access, notes for the video teachings, discussion questions, and personal Bible studies in between group meetings. A leader's best practices and guide is found at the back of each study guide.

FACILITATION

Depending on how your group is formatted, you may need to appoint a person to serve as a facilitator. This person will be responsible for starting the video and keeping track of time during discussions. Facilitators should be prepared to read the discussion questions aloud and to monitor discussions, encouraging everyone in the group to engage and ensuring that everyone has the opportunity to participate.

PERSONAL STUDIES

Between group meetings, maximize the impact of this study on Advent by working through the personal Bible study section. Treat each personal Bible study like committed time with the Lord and your Bible in whatever way works best for your schedule. Allowing time across multiple days provides the greatest opportunity for marinating in God's Word as well as letting the teaching take root. These personal studies are not intended to be burdensome or time-consuming but to help you apply the learned lessons to your everyday, personal life for growth and connection.

SCRIPTURE CUTOUT ARTWORK

We have selected four specific verses from the Bible that carry the Advent narrative as we can experience it today. Each verse page is designed to be cut out and will fit in a standard 8x10 matte frame. Our hope is that you will be reminded of the marvel and miracle of Advent, the wonder of Jesus living with us, all throughout the year.

We have a Savior who is with us.
He is not a faraway God.

— LISA HARPER

The Longing in the Silence

Video

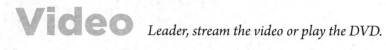

Leader, stream the video or play the DVD.

As you watch, take notes on anything that stands out to you.

> **SCRIPTURE:** Malachi 1:1–2, 2:17, 3:1

Dietrich Bonhoeffer

Malachi

Four hundred years of silence

Rhetorical disputation

The stockings

Under the bed

VOCABULARY	DEFINITION
ADVENT	word with Latin roots, meaning "coming"
PASSOVER	most important Hebrew feast, commemorating their deliverance from Egyptian bondage
PENTECOST	also called the Feast of Weeks, derived from the Greek word meaning "fifty"; occurs fifty days after Passover, and celebrates the end of the grain harvest
FEAST OF THE TABERNACLES	combined the ingathering of the labor of the field (Exodus 23:16), the fruit of the earth (Leviticus 23:39), the ingathering of the threshing floor and winepress (Deuteronomy 16:13), and the dwelling in booths (or tabernacles), which were to be joyful reminders to Israel
RHETORICAL DISPUTATION	dialogue between two parties without specific resolution; dialogue between the Lord and the people of Israel
INTERTESTAMENTAL PERIOD	the period between the end of the Old Testament (Malachi) and the beginning of the ministry of John the Baptist; also known as four hundred years of silence; Jews believe prophecy ceased during this period

Group Discussion

1. **Think about your personal experience with Advent. Perhaps you are hearing the definition for the first time today, or, like Chris, your family had clear and specific Advent traditions.**

    • Did you celebrate it as a child?

    • Do you celebrate it today?

    • What is your understanding of the season?

2. **Ask a volunteer to read Malachi 1:1–2 and 2:17 aloud, and then discuss the following.**

    • In light of the journey God's people have been on, why do you think the Israelites doubt and question God's love?

    • What situations or events cause you to doubt and question God's love?

    • Where do you most need to experience God's love during this Advent season?

3. **After the book of Malachi and the renewed promise of a Savior, God remained silent for four hundred years.**

    • What do you think that silence was like for the Israelites?

    • Where do you feel you're experiencing silence from God in your life?

    • What is the most challenging aspect of this for you?

    • How have you seen God working in the silence?

    • How does recognizing and contemplating periods of God's silence deepen your appreciation of waiting for the coming of Christ we celebrate during Advent?

- Where do you feel like you've been waiting, for what seems like forever, for God to answer a desire?

- In what ways might you trust God with that desire this Advent season?

4. **Lisa tells the story of decorating for Christmas and hanging precious stockings for Missy's arrival only to be told that she would probably never be able to bring Missy home.**

> *"I took down every single light, every single ornament, and I packed them all up in cardboard boxes. I shoved them under my stairs and thought, I'll never celebrate Christmas again. This was just too hard."*

- What are some reasons we might hold back from hope or from asking God for something we long for?

5. **The intertestamental period is calculated to be fourteen generations, according to Daniel 9:24–27. Consider what you know about the lives of your ancestors.**

- Do you know what your grandparents hoped for just two generations from you? What they prayed and trusted God for?

- How difficult do you think it is to carry on a shared hope for the exact same thing for fourteen generations? What might happen to the understanding of what is being hoped for?

- How do you think the Israelites handled the hope for the promise God made that a Savior was coming who would make all things right through fourteen generations of people? What were their tactics for maintaining collective hope?

- In light of today's teaching, how are you currently thinking of ways to share your hope in Jesus with other generations?

Holding on to hope in our Savior is as equally important as sharing our hope with others.

6. **Though God's people are frustrated, disappointed, and angry that life hasn't turned out like they expected, God promises a Savior. He tells them Christ is coming, right around the corner. Select a volunteer to read Malachi 3:1 and discuss the following.**

- What words or phrases are most meaningful to you from this passage?

- Why does it matter to God's people, and us today, that He is coming?

- What prevents you from believing that Jesus can come into your greatest disappointment, fear, doubt, or wonder?

7. **Lisa tells the story of hiding under her bed after she wrecked her bike and her mother crawling underneath the bed to be with her.**

> *"That's the promise of Advent, y'all. No matter where we are, even when we've wedged ourselves in some dark place because we're so disappointed, God pursues us. He's so kind, and He's with us. Wherever you are this Advent season, you are not invisible to Him."*

- Describe a time when you were in a dark place and someone lovingly pursued you.

- What did that feel like? What made it meaningful?

- What do you hope for most from celebrating Advent?

Call to Action

Leader, you will need some pieces of paper, about a quarter- or half-page for this exercise.

Pass out a piece of paper to each group member. Invite each participant to write down something they are longing for or hoping for this Advent season. Place each slip of paper into a bowl or basket and mix them up. Then have each person draw one and pray over that longing or hope for the next week.

Closing Prayer

Select a volunteer to read the closing prayer over the group.

Lord Jesus, nothing is hidden from You. Strengthen our resolve to remain hopeful even when we can't see or hear the responses we desire. Help us to share our hope with others who may not know what to hope in. Fill us with holy anticipation of You and Your goodness. In Jesus' name. Amen.

Personal Study

This section is created as a guide to personally study and further explore the experience of Advent and longing in silence.

Don't forget to pray over the longing of one of your fellow group members throughout this week.

LESSON ONE

Advent invites us to pull away from the hectic consumerism that often overtakes the four weeks before Christmas and enter a time of preparation and anticipation for the arrival of Jesus.

✳ What's one meaningful way you've prepared your heart for Christmas in the past?

Throughout the world, believers celebrate this season in beautifully diverse ways. In the heart of Germany, as the Advent season unfolds its tapestry of anticipation, families gather around a wreath with four candles. Each week, families encircle the wreath and light a candle which casts its warm glow upon those gathered, a beacon of hope and joy.

Across the expanse of Mexico, you'll find a nine-day religious ceremony known as Las Posadas, or "The Inns," held throughout towns and villages. It's held from December 16–24 to celebrate the journey of Mary and Joseph. In the evening, a child dressed as an angel leads a group of other children to selected homes where they are not allowed entry but still given refreshments.

In China, believers illuminate their homes using colorful paper lanterns during the Advent season. Similarly, in the United Kingdom, they make Christingles, oranges decorated with a red table, candles, and sweets. They also hold Christingles services, which involve readings, singing, prayers, and fundraisers for those in need.

Eastern Orthodox churches celebrate Advent on the Revised Julian Calendar starting November 15 through December 24. They prepare their hearts and minds for Christ's arrival through the Nativity Fast. Participants may abstain from particular foods, including fish, meat, dairy products, and olive oil, for the weeks leading up to Christmas. [1]

All of these practices help participants engage in a hope-filled anticipation of Christ's arrival.

✦ Which of these practices from around the world intrigues you the most? Why?

✦ Which of these practices (or others) would help you engage in this biblical season of waiting?

---

[1] Forrest Brown, "What Is Advent? And What Traditions Do People Follow Worldwide?" November 14, 2023.

> *God doesn't say, "You can only bring perky, happy clappy to Me." But He says, "When you're disappointed, when you don't get what you want... bring that to Me."*

In this season of Advent, where do you most need to get honest with God?

What do you need to surrender to God?

What doubts do you need to give to God?

✛ What are the disappointments you need God's healing and restoration for?

✛ What do you most want to receive from God during this season of Advent?

In the space below, write a prayer that surrenders your hesitations, fears, disappointments, doubts, and pain. Then ask God to fill you with hope-filled anticipation for how He might meet and renew you during Advent.

LESSON TWO

We can easily open the Gospels and discover stunning accounts of Jesus' birth and the layers of miracles surrounding His arrival. Though Jesus' entrance into this world comes quickly to us, we must remember that God's people had been longing for the promised deliverer for thousands of years, and the wait was often uncomfortable and hard.

After seventy brutal years in Babylonian captivity, God's people returned home to Jerusalem with sky-high hopes. They planned to rebuild their lives, worship in the temple, and experience the goodness of God that all the prophets had promised. They were convinced that with their new freedom, the Messiah would soon return, establish His holy reign, and deliver justice, peace, and abundance for all.

Alas, their hopes were soon dashed. The temple they planned to worship and celebrate in had been demolished. Much of their great city had been reduced to rubble. And worse, the long-awaited Messiah was nowhere to be found.

Life didn't turn out like they'd hoped or planned. For the next hundred years, God's people flourished in their population but floundered in their faith. Injustice and corruption abounded. And their hearts turned to stone.

Around a century after their escape from Babylon, the prophet Malachi, whose name means "messenger," arrives in their midst. He's been sent by God to expose and confront the hardness of the people's hearts. What unfolds is a series of six rhetorical disputes. God makes a claim, and the Israelites either protest or debate the claim.

Read Malachi 1:2.

+ What claim does God make, and what question do the people ask?

"You are precious to Him. That's the promise of Malachi. That's a promise from Genesis to Revelation. We have a Savior who's with us; He's not a faraway God."

God goes on to remind the people of the promises He made to Jacob instead of Esau (or who would become Edom), who eventually came to ruin. God has kept the promise of His love for them throughout the generations.

+ When are you most tempted to doubt or question God's love?

✦ How do you tend to treat God's guidance and instruction when you don't trust His love? Does your typical response bear fruit or leave you still in need? What might need to change?

✦ Where do you most need to know the depths of God's love and favor in your life right now?

Read Jeremiah 31:3 and Zephaniah 3:17.

✦ What do each of these passages reveal about the nature of God's love for you?

The book of Malachi goes on to reveal that the time in exile didn't soften the hearts of God's people or lead to lasting repentance. So, God meets the people in their frustration and refusal to obey, exposes the hardness of their hearts, and calls them to return to Him.

READ	BEHAVIOR GOD CALLS OUT IN THE ISRAELITES	BEHAVIOR GOD CALLS OUT IN ME
Malachi 1:6–2:9		
Malachi 2:10–16		
Malachi 2:17–3:5		
Malachi 3:6–12		
Malachi 3:13–18		

✦ What does it reveal about God that He calls people back to Himself no matter how far they've wandered?

✦ Where do you sense God calling you to return to Him?

Now remember that this riveting conversation between God and His people, known as the book of Malachi, is the final book of the Old Testament. These questions, doubts, and struggles are the last thing God wants to address before the centuries of silence that will follow.

And tucked into this dialogue is a stunning promise regarding the One who is yet to come.

Read Malachi 3:1–4.

+ What stands out to you about the promised Messiah?

Malachi predicts the arrival of John the Baptist (3:1), who prepares the way for the Lord (Mark 1:1–4), and that Jesus, as the Refiner, will fulfill God's promises. This is incredible news! But it's also a promise that must be held on to for four hundred years before it's fulfilled—as we'll discover in the next lesson of personal study.

* * *

LESSON THREE

In the final book of the Old Testament, Malachi, we receive the powerful anchor of hope of the coming Christ. Yet centuries of uncomfortable silence followed. We have the privilege now of knowing that period between the Old and New Testaments lasted four hundred years, but the generations who lived and died during those centuries had no idea when it would end. The prophets of God had vanished. The voice of God had gone silent. And the people were left in a great unknowing of when God might speak to them again, let alone fulfill His promise of the long-awaited Messiah.

It is in this very silence we are invited to wait and pray and anticipate and long for God. That's one of the great gifts of Advent: It gives space for reflective preparation of what God has done and is yet to do.

Which of the following have you felt or faced when you're waiting on God and all you hear is silence? Circle all that apply.

Disappointed	Frustrated	Expectant
Angry	Disoriented	Questioning
Hopeful	Afraid	Confused
Doubtful	Disillusioned	Sad

All of these are normal human responses, and all have been experienced by God's people for thousands of years. Yet rather than become stuck in our disappointment or disorientation, we can use the time to reorient ourselves toward Jesus and increase our dependence on God.

One of the rich places in the Bible where we find both our heartaches and sacred hopes expressed side by side is throughout the Psalms.

Read the following passages. What does each one reveal about God's character and His trustworthiness even in the silence and even when we can't see the outcome?

SCRIPTURE	WHAT IS REVEALED ABOUT THE CHARACTER OF GOD?
Psalm 9:7–10	
Psalm 40:4–5	
Psalm 91:1–6	
Psalm 112:6–9	
Psalm 143:8–10	

✦ **As you review the chart, which characteristic of God are you struggling to trust most now?**

Write a prayer of response asking God to renew your trust in who He is and His faithfulness.

"You know what God is saying to His disappointed people... 'Christmas is coming. Christmas is coming, Emmanuel. He's right around the corner.'"

In this season of Advent, we all have areas where we're waiting for God to break the silence and for Christ to come anew. What are three areas where you're waiting for God to break the silence and for Christ to come and heal, restore, or make all things new?

✴ What are you leaning on to fulfill these desires other than God?

✴ What steps can you take to remove those from your life during the upcoming weeks of Advent?

This whole season of Advent is a time of waiting, a time of preparing, a time of reorienting.

— CHRISTINE CAINE

The Practice of Hopeful Waiting

Video Leader, stream the video or play the DVD.

As you watch, take notes on anything that stands out to you.

SCRIPTURE: Luke 1:39–45

Struggles with waiting and patience

Mary and Elizabeth

Two angelic visitations and two supernatural pregnancies

Zechariah

A21 Organization

Group Discussion

1. **Like so many of us, Christine confesses that she struggles with waiting and patience.**

   - On a scale of one to ten, with one being not at all and ten being very much, how much do you struggle with waiting and patience?

   - How does Advent, a season of waiting and preparing, help reorient you toward patience for the promises of God to be fulfilled?

2. **Christine observes that we're living between the two Advents—the arrival of Jesus at His birth and the return of Jesus at His second coming. What does it look like for you to wait well in the in-between?**

   - God's revelation or miracle in our lives not only comes at His time, but it also comes over time—and it's rarely what we expect.

   - Describe a time when God answered your prayer, but it wasn't in the timeframe or way that you expected.

   - How can we believe for something beyond our expectations?

3. **Select a few volunteers to read Luke 1:5–14 and Luke 1:24–25, and discuss the following.**

   - How did Elizabeth remain faithful in the midst of unmet expectations?

   - What miracle are you waiting for?

   - What is your response to waiting for the miracle?

   - What do you anticipate your response will be to receiving the miracle?

"What I have discovered is that what is impossible with men is possible with God. It's just likely to take longer than we expect. But too often we look at our own natural limitations instead of trusting God and His supernatural ability. When God breaks the silence after four hundred years, it's so supernatural—two angel visitations and two miraculous pregnancies. For both Mary and Elizabeth, it was the appointed time. God will give us what we need at the appointed time—it's just that usually the timing of our appointed time and God's appointed time don't align."

4. **Consider how your personal experiences or disappointments might have limited what you believe God can do in your life.**

    - What does it look like for you to wait on God well?

    - What situation might you be facing where your appointed time and God's appointed time are not in alignment?

    - How do you suspect God might be working in the waiting?

5. **Select a few volunteers to read Luke 1:36–50 and Luke 1:56, and discuss the following.**

    - How does Elizabeth respond to Mary and Mary respond to Elizabeth?

    - How do they celebrate rather than compare their miracles?

    - What lesson can be found in their interactions and the way they support each other?

    - Who is someone you can celebrate and encourage who is experiencing his or her miracle? Or someone who is still waiting on God?

6. **"Nothing will be impossible with God" (Luke 1:37), but sometimes after years of silence and waiting, we grow impatient and feel like some things are impossible.**

- What have you given up on that you can start praying for again during Advent?

- How can you lean into Jesus for what only He can do?

Call to Action

Leader, you will need some pieces of paper, about a quarter- or half-page for this exercise.

Pass out a piece of paper to each group member. Invite each participant to write down where they most need God to do what feels impossible. Place each slip of paper into a bowl or basket and mix them up. Then have each person draw one and pray over that request, asking for a renewal of hope over the next week.

Closing Prayer

Select a volunteer to read the closing prayer over the group.

Lord Jesus, nothing is impossible for You. But sometimes in the waiting and the longing, we struggle to hold on to greater faith. Help our unbelief. Strengthen our resolve to trust You and Your timing with everything. Help us to wait well. May we be like Elizabeth and Mary. May we support each other and celebrate the work You're doing in all our lives. May we remain faithful in prayer. May we experience You doing the impossible. In Jesus' name. Amen.

Personal Study

Check in with your group members during the upcoming week. Don't forget to pray for the impossible for one of your group members.

* * *

LESSON ONE

God's people didn't know when the promised Savior would arrive or what form He would take, but His arrival would change the course of history. The Deliverer would come to God's people and be a leader like no other. Throughout the Old Testament, we find descriptions, allusions, prophecies, and even foreshadowing of the long-anticipated Messiah who would rescue God's people and set all things right. And there's even prophecy regarding Elizabeth and Zechariah's son, John the Baptist.

Read Daniel 7:13–14 and Luke 1:31–33.

✳ What is prophesied about the Messiah?

✳ How is this specifically fulfilled through Jesus' arrival?

Read Isaiah 7:14 and Luke 1:35.

✦ What is prophesied about the Messiah?

✦ How is this specifically fulfilled through Jesus' arrival?

Read Micah 5:2 and Matthew 2:4–7.

✦ What is prophesied about the Messiah?

✦ How is this specifically fulfilled through Jesus' arrival?

Read Isaiah 40:3–5 and Matthew 3:1–3.

✦ What is prophesied about John the Baptist?

✦ How is this specifically fulfilled through John the Baptist's arrival and life?

"Had Elizabeth gotten pregnant any earlier, it wouldn't have been the right time. So many times things happen and you look back and go, 'Wow, God's timing was so right.'"

✦ How is God's timing perfect with the arrival of John the Baptist and Jesus within months of each other?

+ In what circumstances is it easy for you to trust God's perfect timing?

+ When is it most challenging for you to trust God's perfect timing? Why do you think this/these circumstances make trusting God's timing more difficult?

Which of the following best describes your attitude toward waiting on God for the impossible? Circle all that apply.

Humble	Patient	Angry
Frustrated	Peaceful	Joyful
Bitter	Grateful	Hopeful

＊ Consider the attitudes you circled. How is your attitude affecting your relationship with God? Is your attitude fostering a closer relationship or causing distance? What needs to change?

What do the following passages reveal about what God wants to give you as you wait on Him?

＊ Lamentations 3:25:

＊ Psalm 27:14:

＊ Isaiah 30:18:

In the space below, write a prayer asking God to give you all these things and to guide and help your attitude as you wait on Him.

"God's promise and purpose for our lives will come at the appointed time. It's just that God's appointed time and our timing don't always align."

✦ As we embrace this season of Advent, where are you most frustrated with God's timing?

✦ Where do you sense God is telling you to be patient and trust His perfect timing?

LESSON TWO

Elizabeth was the descendent of a line of priests who traced back to Aaron. She grew up in a priestly home, and she married a priest. Yet despite her faithfulness, she remained barren. In antiquity, infertility was viewed as a sign that God was punishing you for your sins. Beyond the disappointment of not being able to conceive, Elizabeth lived with public shame for her barrenness, yet she had done nothing wrong.

Read Luke 1:5–7, and fill in the chart below.

WORDS AND PHRASES USED TO DESCRIBE ZECHARIAH	WORDS AND PHRASES USED TO DESCRIBE ELIZABETH

✴ Reflecting on the chart, why was it extra painful for the couple to be infertile?

✴ In what area of your life have you done everything you know to do but circumstances haven't yet turned out like you're hoping?

✴ How have you responded to this disappointment?

Read Luke 1:8–17.

✦ What does the angel tell Zechariah about his son?

✦ How is the angel's news better than anything Zechariah could have imagined?

✦ What are three desires you're prayerfully waiting on God to fulfill?

 1

 2

 3

Ephesians 3:20–21 says, "Now to him who is able to do above and beyond all that we ask or think according to the power that works in us—to him be glory in the church and in Christ Jesus to all generations, forever and ever. Amen."

✦ Do you expect God to fulfill what you're longing for or to do something beyond all that you can hope or imagine? Why?

✦ How was the arrival of Christ something that went beyond all that anyone could ever hope or imagine?

"We often only see our little piece of the puzzle. We get so frustrated and God says, 'Oh, I'm orchestrating something so much bigger!'"

Think about something you've previously waited on or are still waiting on the Lord for. Use whatever comes to mind to consider these questions.

✦ One of the hidden gifts of waiting is that God is still working all around you and even in you. How have you seen Him continue to work around you and in you, even in the midst of waiting?

✦ Has your waiting been a type of refining process for you? Explain.

✦ What has waiting exposed about you and what you really believe?

✦ How does waiting increase your dependence on God?

✦ In what ways have you become more Christlike through seasons of waiting?

In the space below, write a prayer of gratitude for the season of waiting that you're currently in and what God is accomplishing through it.

LESSON THREE

Jesus performed countless miracles during His earthly ministry, but the miracles began before He was born! Have you ever considered just how many miracles surrounded Jesus' birth?

Read Luke 1:5–80. In the space below, make notes of all the miracles you see.

+ What does the abundance of miracles reveal about how God might be working in our season of Advent and waiting on the Christ child's arrival?

✦ How might previous disappointments or hurts be preventing you from recognizing the miraculous work God is doing in your life right now?

Read Proverbs 13:12.

✦ How have your deferred hopes made you feel heartsick?

"We limit God to what we can see, taste, touch, smell, feel, and hear—all our personal experiences, our disappointments or our discouragement. We look at the natural realm, and we limit God to the natural realm."

✦ How can you begin to trust that God can do the impossible and turn things around?

✦ Zechariah, Elizabeth, and Mary remind us that faith is predicated on trust, not understanding. What does it look like right now, in this Advent season, for you to trust in the Lord with all your heart and lean not on your own understanding (Proverbs 3:5–6)?

✦ How do the miracles of Advent challenge you to wait well . . . before you experience God doing the impossible?

In the space below, courageously write out a miracle that you want to see God do through the presence and power of Jesus in this Advent season. Then pray and ask Him to do it!

*The good news is that perfection
is not a prerequisite for those of
us who celebrate Advent.*

LISA HARPER

Emmanuel: God With All of Us

Video

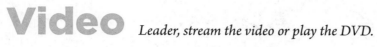

Leader, stream the video or play the DVD.

As you watch, take notes on anything that stands out to you.

SCRIPTURE: Matthew 1:1–6

Missy's bagel

Differences between the Gospels

Tamar

Rahab

Bathsheba

Ruth

Group Discussion

1. **Lisa tells the funny story of Missy and her bagel mishap.**

   • Where have you missed an opportunity to emulate Jesus during the Advent season?

   • What's your response to the following statement: "Perfect is not a prerequisite for those of us who get to celebrate Advent"?

2. **Ask a few participants to read Matthew 1:1–6, and discuss the following.**

   • Why is it significant that the genealogy of Jesus includes women's names?

   • Have you ever examined your own genealogy or ancestry?

   • If so, what surprising characters are in your family line?

   • What does it reveal about God's character that those who were outliers, dismissed, and deemed less than are included in the family of Jesus?

3. **Consider the women in Jesus' genealogy.**

   • What does it reveal about God that Tamar, who disguised herself as a sex worker and slept with her father-in-law, and Rahab, an actual sex worker, are listed in Jesus' family tree?

   • What does it reveal about God that Bathsheba, who was forced into adultery, and Ruth, a Moabite, are listed in Jesus' family tree?

   • Who have you been tempted to overlook or exclude from Jesus' family because of what they they've done or left undone?

4. **Lisa teaches that followers of the Jewish religion had to obey all 613 laws of the Torah perfectly to have any chance of accessing God. They thought they had to be perfect to relate to God and to know Him.**

    • In what ways do you struggle with perfection in everyday life?

    • In what ways do you struggle with perfection in your relationship with Jesus?

    • What changes for you in this season of anticipating the coming Christ when you realize Jesus came for you in spite of your imperfections?

"The entire story of Advent through Matthew's genealogy is about our sovereign, merciful God who didn't demand that we get ourselves together so we could be reconciled to Him. It's just a merciful, transient, holy God who descends to not just be eminent but to be Emmanuel, God with us—even when we're at our very worst—and that's the most wonderful Christmas gift you've ever heard."

5. Consider God's merciful holiness.

    • Where in your life do you believe you still need to "get yourself together" before you can come to God?

    • What do you feel when you hear the description of God's effort to be with us—regardless of our worst?

6. **Lisa talked about Boaz becoming Ruth's kinsman-redeemer. She described Boaz coming to Ruth and saying, "You don't have to glean grain anymore. You don't have to take up the posture of a slave anymore. I'll take care of you." Consider your own history or current situation.**

- What does it mean for you to know Jesus is your Kinsman Redeemer? That Jesus willingly steps into your messy life and says, "I'm here to take care of you"?

- How does this Christmas season change for you knowing the whole story is about Jesus coming for you so that you never have to know a "posture of slavery again"?

Call to Action

Leader, you will need some pieces of paper, about a quarter- or half-page for this exercise.

Pass out a piece of paper to each group member. Invite each participant to write down an area in which they need to experience God's redemption and mercy. Place each slip of paper into a bowl or basket and mix them up. Then have each person draw one and pray over that need this week.

Closing Prayer

Select a volunteer to read the closing prayer over the group.

Lord Jesus, thank You for Advent this season, where You reach down from glory and You put Your holy hands on either side of our faces, and You tilt our attention and our affection back toward You. You tell us of Your love again and again. You remind us that even at our worst, You love us so much. Help us to receive Your grace and mercy in every area of our lives. In Jesus' name. Amen.

Personal Study

Don't forget to pray over your group member and where they need to know redemption and mercy this week.

LESSON ONE

When Advent first started around the fourth century, it was designed as a forty-day time before Christmas to prepare new believers for baptism at the January feast of Epiphany, a celebration of God's incarnation. Early Christians marked this time with prayer and fasting. It wasn't until many centuries later that the season was explicitly linked to Christ's arrival and the celebration of Christmas.

✦   In what ways have you thought of or experienced Advent differently so far this season?

One of the gifts of Advent is the opportunity to visit the story of Christ's arrival with fresh eyes. One of the most profound elements of the genealogy in Matthew is the inclusion of women. In antiquity, women had no standing in society without a man. Everything was passed through the male bloodline, yet Jesus named women in His bloodline—and not just women but women of ill repute.

✦   How does this expand your understanding of Jesus coming for everyone?

+ What is the impact of God breaking four hundred years of silence by upending so many commonly held beliefs among His people?

+ How does this demonstrate the intention of Jesus to draw all people to Himself?

The first woman listed in Matthew's genealogy is Tamar, the daughter-in-law of Judah, one of the sons of Jacob. After Tamar's husband, Er, died, his brother Onan was responsible for marrying her and providing a child. But Onan refused to impregnate her and died. Judah promised that Tamar could marry his youngest son but then did not fulfill his promise.

Read Genesis 38:1–14.

+ How is Tamar repeatedly treated unjustly?

✦ What does Judah's behavior toward Tamar reveal about how women were seen in society?

Feeling abandoned and desperate for offspring to carry on the family line, Tamar devises a plan.

Read Genesis 38:15–26.

✦ How did Tamar outsmart Judah?

✦ What do you think motivated Tamar to take such drastic measures to ensure she had a child?

How did Tamar demonstrate faith, strength, and courage in the face of injustice?

In what ways does Tamar's story challenge your understanding of women in the Bible?

"The entire story is about this sovereign, merciful God who didn't demand that we get ourselves together so we could be reconciled to Him."

✦ What does Tamar's inclusion in Jesus' family tree reveal about God's redemption and grace?

✦ Where do you most need to experience God's redemption and grace in this season of Advent?

LESSON TWO

Another surprising name in Jesus' family tree is a Canaanite woman named Rahab. She lived in Jericho, a city about to be attacked and conquered by God's people. Under the leadership of Joshua, a pair of spies were sent out as military scouts. When they scouted out the land, they lodged at Rahab's house. Rahab, recognizing that the Israelites' God was powerful, hid the spies from the king of Jericho's men and helped them escape by letting them down through a window in the city wall.

Read Joshua 2:1–14.

✦ How does Rahab demonstrate courage and strength in the midst of uncertainty? What makes her a hero?

✦ What led Rahab to help the spies despite the high risk to herself and her family?

Rahab is labeled a prostitute. We all have labels or words—whether we speak them over ourselves or others speak them over us—that make us feel less than.

✳ What label or word has been spoken over you that makes you feel less than?

Those labels are given by humans, not by God. Look up the following passages, and consider what God calls you. Fill in the chart below.

SCRIPTURE	WHAT GOD CALLS YOU
John 1:12	
John 15:15	
Romans 8:17	
2 Corinthians 5:17, 21	
Ephesians 1:4–7	
Ephesians 2:10	

What human labels do you need to replace with the truth of what God calls you? Write a prayer in the space below asking God to free you from any untruths about who you are and fill you with the truth of who He says you are.

Read Joshua 2:15–24 and Joshua 6:22–23.

+ What pact do the spies make with Rahab, and how do they fulfill it?

✦ How does Rahab's assistance to the spies lead to her own salvation?

✦ How does Rahab defy stereotypes of women then and today?

✦ Which characteristic makes it more shocking that Rahab is in Jesus' family tree—that she was a Canaanite or that she was a prostitute?

✦ How does Rahab's story encourage those who feel marginalized or like outsiders?

Bathsheba was the wife of Uriah the Hittite, a loyal soldier serving in King David's army. While bathing on the rooftop of her house, King David caught sight of her from his palace and wanted her for himself, even though she was married. David called for her to come to the palace, and he slept with her. She soon became pregnant. To conceal the affair, David called Uriah back from the battlefield and encouraged him to be with his wife. Uriah's loyalty to his fellow soldiers, nation, and king was too great, and he refused to engage in the marital pleasure.

David then sent Uriah to the front lines of battle where he was killed. David married Bathsheba, and she gave birth to a son, but the child died.

Read 2 Samuel 11:1–5.

✳ What power dynamics are at play between the king and Bathsheba?

✳ How does Bathsheba's lack of choice in this story impact your understanding of her character?

Read 2 Samuel 11:14–16 and 2 Samuel 11:23–26.

✳ What is the impact of David's actions on Bathsheba and her family?

After Bathsheba and David lose their child, they eventually have another son, Solomon, who becomes one of the greatest kings of Israel.

Jesus essentially said: "The least of these, the most mistake-prone of these, the ones that you look down your nose at, are the ones I'll not just claim as Mine, I'll actually, in My sovereignty, weave them into the literal family tree of My very own Son."

Read Matthew 1:6.

✴ What does it reveal about God's redemptive purposes that Bathsheba would be included in Jesus' family tree?

✴ What do the stories of Rahab and Bathsheba reveal to you about God's redeeming love?

✴ Where do you most need to experience His redeeming love in your life?

— LESSON THREE —

The fourth woman, Ruth, mentioned in Jesus' family tree in Matthew is a Moabite. Now, the Moabites were a people group who started by incest. After fleeing the cities of Sodom and Gomorrah, Lot and his two daughters lived in a cave in the mountains. Lot's daughters devised a plan to take matters into their own hands to preserve their family line.

Read Genesis 19:30–38.

✦ What did Lot's daughters do to preserve their family line?

✦ Why do you think Moabites would feel shame about where they came from for generations?

Centuries later, during a time of famine in Bethlehem, Elimelech, his wife Naomi, and their two sons travel to Moab in order to survive. While there, the two sons marry Moabite women, Ruth and Orpah. Then unspeakable tragedy strikes. Naomi loses her husband and two sons; she and her daughters-in-law become widows.

When Naomi learns the famine has ended, she decides to return home—and Ruth insists on going with her.

Read Ruth 1:12–17.

+ What characteristics does Ruth demonstrate in her response to Naomi?

+ How are Ruth's words a confession of faith in God?

+ How does Ruth's response to Naomi challenge the way you think about family?

What family members most need your prayer and love this Advent season? Write their names below and write a prayer next to each one.

NAME	PRAYER

To support her mother-in-law, Ruth gleans the fields of a wealthy relative named Boaz. As she gathers the leftover grain for the harvest, Boaz shows her kindness and protection. Naomi devises a plan to help Boaz recognize his significance as a possible kinsman-redeemer, or one who can marry Ruth. After another relative declines the opportunity, Ruth and Boaz marry.

Read Ruth 4:13–16.

✦   How do Ruth and Naomi find healing and restoration?

Read Deuteronomy 23:3.

✦   What shame or embarrassment do you suspect Ruth might have felt or experienced from being a Moabite?

✦ What in your family has caused you shame or embarrassment?

✦ What does it reveal about God that He would rescue Ruth through Boaz, and include Ruth, the Moabite, in the genealogy of King David and Jesus Christ?

✦ What does it suggest about God's plan and redemption for you and your family?

✦ What's your greatest insecurity with God?

✴ How do the stories of Tamar, Rahab, Bathsheba, and Ruth challenge you to let go of any insecurities and receive God's love?

✴ What changes for you this Advent season knowing sex workers were included and named in God's plan of redemption? And that you too are intentionally included in His plan?

Anna didn't run from God; she ran toward Him, and she saw the promise because she didn't give up.

CHRISTINE CAINE

This Is Just the Beginning

Video 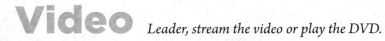 *Leader, stream the video or play the DVD.*

As you watch, take notes on anything that stands out to you.

SCRIPTURE: Luke 2:21–38

Mary adhered to the law

Simeon

God uses women

Anna

Well along in years

Tragic accident

Group Discussion

1. **Do you tend to think that your best years are behind you or ahead of you?**

   • How does Anna's story challenge or support your thinking?

   • How has your faith changed as you've aged?

2. **Invite a participant to read Luke 2:36–38 aloud, and discuss the following.**

   • When you encounter loss or disappointment, like Anna becoming a widow, do you tend to run toward God or away from God? Explain.

   • What characteristic in Anna's life would you most want to have in your own?

   • How does Anna's devotion to prayer and fasting shape her understanding of God and her presence in the temple?

   • How does Anna's story contribute to the broader narrative of Jesus' birth and fulfillment of God's promises?

3. **Consider the age and life experience difference between Anna and Mary.**

   • How does God use the connection between a more mature woman (Anna) and a young woman (Mary) to strengthen both of their faiths?

   • How does being friends with people of different ages strengthen and fortify your faith?

"All of us have the baton of faith in our hands, and it is our job to carry the baton of faith from one generation to the next generation. I know the world has got this whole sort of theory about retirement. I don't see retirement anywhere in the Bible. I just see 'refirement.'"

4. Consider the women in your life.

- Can you name someone who has passed the baton of faith to you, or who has inspired your faith by her own? How has knowing her or observing her affected the way you think of your own faith?

- What are you doing now, or might you begin to do, to carry and pass the baton of faith to the next generation?

- Do you tend to see the final years of your life as retirement or "refirement"? Explain. Where might you change your perspective and realize a "refirement" in your life today?

5. Jesus invited His disciples to "come and see," but the women throughout the Bible are nudged by the Holy Spirit to "go and tell."

- What does it look like for you to go and tell and to share your faith in everyday life?

6. **What has been most meaningful for you during this season of Advent thus far?**

   • How has your heart been prepared for the arrival of the Christ child?

   • How has this season of Advent made you more expectant for Jesus to do the impossible in your life?

Call to Action

Leader, you will need some pieces of paper, about a quarter- or half-page for this exercise.

Pass out a piece of paper to each group member. Invite each participant to write down what they are most grateful for throughout this Advent season. Place each slip of paper into a bowl or basket and mix them up. Then have each person draw one. Go around the group and read each statement aloud as a group prayer of thanks.

Closing Prayer

Select a volunteer to read the closing prayer over the group.

Lord Jesus, thank You for this incredible season where we have the opportunity to prepare our hearts for Your arrival into this world and into our lives anew. Help us to carry and pass the baton of faith well. Help us to be faithful and true to You. Help us to go and tell everyone the good news about You. We are so grateful for You. We love You. In Jesus' name. Amen.

Personal Study

Remember to pray in full gratitude and
expectation for your whole group this
week, praising God and thanking Him
for sending Jesus.

LESSON ONE

The miracles surrounding Jesus' birth are breathtaking. From the miracle of the announcement to Mary to the miracle of Elizabeth becoming pregnant in her old age, we see that nothing is impossible for God. But the miracles didn't just come to Mary and Joseph and their family; they came to those who had spent their lives waiting for the Messiah's arrival. Mary and Joseph, just like any faithful Jewish couple, honored the religious laws regarding their child's birth. After Jesus' birth, the time came for Him to be presented at the temple.

Read Exodus 13:12–15.

✳ What does this passage reveal about the ceremony of the presentation of the firstborn?

Read Leviticus 12:1–8.

✳ What does this passage reveal about the ceremony of purification for Mary?

Read Luke 2:22–24.

✦ Why did Mary and Joseph bring Jesus to the temple? What does this passage reveal about Mary and Joseph's finances that they offered a pair of birds for a sacrifice rather than a lamb?

✦ What does Mary and Joseph's obedience to God's laws reveal about their character?

✦ When Mary and Joseph enter the temple, they meet Simeon, a man who has been faithfully waiting on God to fulfill a promise for many years.

"God is always faithful and His work in our lives doesn't often happen how we think. BUT! It's going to happen . . . God makes all things happen in His timing."

Read Luke 2:25–26.

✦ What does this passage reveal about Simeon?

✦ What is one promise of God that you've been waiting on for years?

✦ What does it look like for you to remain righteous and devout in your waiting?

Read Luke 2:27–35.

✦ How does Simeon respond to God fulfilling His promise?

✦ How do Mary and Joseph respond to Simeon?

✦ How does Simeon's story challenge your expectations of how and when God works in your life?

✦ What does Simeon's story reveal about trusting in God's timing?

✦ What are some ways you can recognize the presence of Jesus in this season of Advent, as Simeon did with the infant Jesus?

* * *

LESSON TWO

While Simeon was prompted by the Spirit to go to the temple (Luke 2:27), Anna spent most of her life in the temple, dedicating her life to worshipping God.

Read Luke 2:36–38.

+ What pain and disappointment had Anna experienced in her life?

+ How did Anna respond to the pain and disappointment?

+ How do you typically respond to pain and disappointment?

✦ What in Anna's story challenges you to respond differently now, than perhaps how you have previously in your life?

✦ What does Anna's story reveal about the perfect timing of God?

"God has always used women. God has always spoken through women. God has always used a woman's voice."

✦ How did Anna's devotion prepare her to recognize Jesus as the Messiah?

+ How does Anna's appointment from God challenge your understanding of who can proclaim the message of Jesus and recognize His presence and work?

We have learned of some pretty remarkable women who have gone before us in Scripture. Reflect on the stories and circumstances of all the women in God's perfectly planned and executed redemption—Tamar (Genesis 38:1-26), Rahab (Joshua 2:1-24; 6:22-23), Ruth (Ruth 1:12-17; 4:13-16), Bathsheba (2 Samuel 11:1-5, 14-16, 23-26), Elizabeth (Luke 1:5-14, 24-25, 36-45, 56), Mary (Luke 1:36-50, 56), Anna (Luke 2:36-38). Consider how their responses to the calls God placed on their lives, in an assortment of circumstances, played a significant role in the coming life we anticipate and celebrate during Advent.

Read the following passage and circle each call to action the author of Hebrews claims over all believers. (Hint: There are three.)

"Therefore, since we also have such a large cloud of witnesses surrounding us, let us lay aside every hindrance and the sin that so easily ensnares us. Let us run with endurance the race that lies before us, keeping our eyes on Jesus, the pioneer and perfecter of our faith." (Hebrews 12:1–2)

Now, write each call to action in the chart below. Fill in how you will respond in the corresponding column.

CALL TO ACTION	HOW I WILL RESPOND

✦ ✦ ✦

LESSON THREE

Advent invites us into a time of celebration of the birth of Jesus for His first arrival, but it also stirs our hearts to anticipate the return of Jesus in His second coming. We live in between when Jesus came and when Jesus will come again.

Read John 6:39–40 and John 14:1–3.

✦ What greatest hope do you find in Jesus' promises?

Read Revelation 21:1–14.

✦ What do you long for most in this description of the new heaven and the new earth that accompanies Christ's second coming?

✦ How has this season of Advent challenged you to remain vigilant and attentive to God's presence and work in your life?

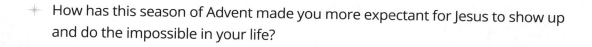

"Jesus has come and He is coming again, and all things will be made new. And that is what we long for. That is the hope of this Advent series. This is why we're not just going through the motions."

✦ How has this season of Advent made you more expectant for Jesus to show up and do the impossible in your life?

✴ How do you feel about Advent now that you have completed this study?

✴ How has your relationship with God changed during this study?

✴ How has your relationship with others changed during this study?

✴ What's your greatest takeaway from this study?

Leader's
Guide

Thank you for your willingness to lead your group through *The Marvel and Miracle of Advent: Recapturing the Wonder of Jesus Living with Us*. The rewards of leading are different from the rewards of participating, and we hope you find your own walk with Jesus deepened by this experience. This leader's guide will give you some tips on how to prepare for your time together and facilitate a meaningful experience for your group members.

WHAT DOES IT TAKE TO LEAD THIS STUDY?

Get together and watch God show up. Seriously, that's the basics of how a small group works. Gather several people together who have a hunger for God, want to learn more about what is in store for them at "the renewal of all things" (Matthew 19:28), and are willing to be open and honest with God and themselves. You don't have to be a pastor, priest, theologian, or counselor to lead a group through this study. Just invite people over, watch the video, and talk about it. All you need is a willing heart, a little courage, and God will do the rest. Really.

HOW THIS STUDY WORKS

There are two important pieces to *The Marvel and Miracle of Advent* small-group study: (1) the four-session video teaching and (2) this study guide. Make sure everyone in your group has a copy of the study guide. The great part is that each study guide includes free access to streaming all of the video teaching.

Each video session is approximately twenty-four minutes in length. When your group meets together, you will watch the video and discuss the session. This study is perfect for home groups, classroom settings, Sunday school classes, and any variety of large- or small-group gathering—though you may need to modify the discussion time depending on the size of the class. Whether you meet weekly, biweekly, watch the videos as a group, watch the videos individually and gather for discussion, or any other format that fits your context, the goal is to share this teaching from Lisa and Chris with others in lively, provocative, and edifying discussions.

A FEW TIPS FOR LEADING A GROUP

The setting really matters. Select an environment that's conducive to people relaxing and getting real. Remember, the Enemy likes to distract us when it comes to seeking closeness to God in any way, so do what you can to remove these obstacles from your group (silence cell phones, limit background noise, no texting).

Have some refreshments! Coffee and water will do; cookies and snacks are even better. People tend to be nervous when they join a new group, so if you can give them something to hold on to (like a warm mug of coffee), they will relax a lot more. It's human nature.

Good equipment is important. Meet where you can watch the video sessions on a screen big enough for everyone to see and enjoy. Get or borrow the best gear you can. Also, be sure to test your media equipment ahead of time to make sure everything is in working condition. This way, if something isn't working, you can fix it or make other arrangements before the meeting begins. (You'll be amazed at how the Enemy will try to mess things up for you!)

Be honest. Remember that your honesty will set the tone for your time together. Be willing to answer questions personally, as this will set the pace for the length of your group members' responses and will make others more comfortable in sharing.

Stick to the schedule. Strive to begin and end at the same time each week. The people in your group are busy, and if they can trust you to be a good steward of their time, they will be more willing to come back each week. Of course, you want to be open to the work God is doing in the group members as they are challenged to reconsider some of their preconceived ideas about Advent and this time leading up to Christ's arrival. At times you may want to linger in discussion. Remember the clock serves you; your group doesn't serve the clock. But work to respect the group's time, especially when it comes to limiting the discussion times.

Don't be afraid of silence or emotion. Welcome awkward moments. The material presented during this study will likely challenge the group members to consider some personal emotions or experiences they have not connected to the season of Advent.

Don't dominate the conversation. Even though you are the leader, you are also a member of this small group. So don't steamroll over others in an attempt to lead—and don't let anyone else in the group do so either.

Prepare for your meeting. Watch the video for the meeting ahead of time. Though it may feel a bit like cheating because you'll know what's coming, you'll be better prepared for what the session might stir in the hearts of your group members. Also review all discussion questions so you are fully prepared for where the conversation may go. Trust the Holy Spirit in guiding you and the discussion time. The most important thing you can do is simply pray ahead of time each week:

> *Lord Jesus, come and rule this time. Let Your Spirit fill this place. Bring Your kingdom here. Take us right to the things we really need to talk about and rescue us from every distraction. Show us Your heart, Father. Meet each of us here. Give us Your grace and love for one another as we learn and grow in anticipation of Your coming here to live with all of us. Thank You in advance. In Your name I pray.*

Make sure your group members are prepared. A week or two before the first meeting send out an email with a reminder to purchase a study guide (available at all online retail sites). Or, secure enough copies for your entire group to hand out at your first gathering. Send out a reminder email or a text a couple of days before the meeting to make sure people don't forget when and where you are meeting.

AS YOU GATHER

You will find the following counsel to be especially helpful when you meet for the first time as a group. We offer these comments in the spirit of "here is what we would do if we were leading a group through this study."

First, as the group gathers, start your time with introductions if people don't know each other. Begin with yourself and share your name, how long you've been a follower of Christ, if you have a spouse and/or children, and what you want to learn most about *The Marvel and Miracle of Advent*. Going first will put the group more at ease.

After each person has introduced themselves, share—in no more than five minutes—what your hopes are for the group. Then jump right in to watching the video session, as this will help get things started on a strong note. In the following weeks you will then want to start by allowing folks to catch up a little—say, five minutes or so. Too much of this burns up your meeting time, but you have to allow some room for it because it helps build relationships among the group members.

Note that each group will have its own personality and dynamics. Typically, people will hold back the first week or two until they feel the group is safe. Then they will begin to share. Again, don't let it throw you if your group seems a bit awkward at first. Of course, some people never want to talk, so you'll need to coax them out as time goes on. But let it go the first week.

INSIGHT FOR DISCUSSION

If the group members are in any way open to talking about their lives as it relates to this material, you will not have enough time for every question suggested in this study guide. That's okay! Pick the questions ahead of time that you know you want to cover, just in case you end up only having time to discuss a few of them.

You set the tone for the group. Your honesty and vulnerability during discussion times will tell them what they can share. How long you talk will give them an example of how long they should. So give some thought to what stories or insights from your own work in the study guide you want to highlight.

WARNING: The greatest temptation for most small-group leaders is to add to the video teaching with a little "teaching session" of their own. This is unhelpful for two reasons:

1. The discussion time will be the richest time during your meeting. The video sessions are the teaching. If you add to the teaching, you sacrifice precious time for discussion and can distract from the intended teaching.

2. You don't want your group members teaching, lecturing, or correcting one another. Every person is at a different place in his or her spiritual journey, and that's good. The best way to encourage productive discussion after a teaching is to begin the conversation straight away with whichever question in this guide you selected to begin with.

A STRONG CLOSE

Some of the best learning times will take place after the group time as God brings new insights to the participants during the week. Encourage group members to write down any questions they have as they do the Bible study work in between group meetings. Make sure they know you are available for them. Take advantage of the activity at the close of each session and encourage group members to pray for the member's request they receive. End your meeting time following either the prompted prayer or having a volunteer pray over your group, and respect this as the official close of your meeting time. This helps establish a set ending and indicates to everyone they are good to go!

Thank you again for taking the time to lead your group. May God reward your efforts and dedication and make your time together in *The Marvel and Miracle of Advent* a true experience of recapturing the wonder of Jesus living with us!

Behold,
I send my messenger,
and he will prepare
the way before me.
*And the Lord
whom you seek*
will suddenly come
to his temple;
and the messenger
of the covenant
in whom you delight,
behold, he is coming,
says the Lord of hosts.

—Malachi 3:1 ESV

For *nothing*
will be
impossible
with God.

—Luke 1:37

For I know
that my

*Redeemer
lives,*

and at the last
he will

stand upon

the earth.

—Job 19:25

At that very moment, she came up and began to thank God and to speak about him to all who were looking forward to the redemption of Jerusalem

—Luke 2:38

About
the Authors

MEET CHRISTINE CAINE +

Christine Caine is a speaker, activist, and bestselling author. She and her husband, Nick, founded The A21 Campaign, an anti–human trafficking organization. They also founded Propel Women, an initiative that is dedicated to coming alongside women all over the globe to activate their God-given purpose. You can tune into Christine's weekly podcast, *Equip & Empower*, or her TBN television program to be encouraged with the hope of Jesus wherever you are. To learn more about Christine, visit www.christinecaine.com.

MEET LISA HARPER +

Lauded as a "hilarious storyteller" and "theological storyteller," Lisa Harper is anything but stereotypical! She is known for emphasizing that accruing knowledge about God pales next to a real and intimate relationship with Jesus. Lisa has 30+ years of church and para-church ministry leadership, as well as a decade speaking on-tour with Women of Faith. She holds a Master of Theological Studies from Covenant Seminary and is in the thesis stage of an earned doctorate at Denver Seminary. She is a regular on TBN's globally syndicated *Better Together* show and has published multiple books and Bible studies. Lisa has also been leading the same weekly Bible study in her neighborhood for fifteen years. The most noticeable thing about Lisa Harper is her authenticity and love for Christ. But her greatest accomplishment to date is getting to become Missy's mom through the miracle of adoption in 2014!

Also Available From Christine

MOVE CONFIDENTLY INTO THE PURPOSE GOD HAS FOR YOU
With a rallying cry to "remember Lot's wife," Christine motivates us to stop looking back, to let go, and to move forward into what God promises for our lives.

FAITH THAT CANNOT BE SHAKEN IS POSSIBLE
Develop a relentless faith so that the next time life throws you a curveball, you will be able to navigate your way through, still living the adventure God planned for you!

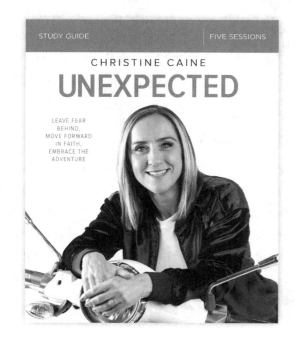

Also Available From Christine

**TODAY IS THE DAY
TO FULFILL YOUR DESTINY**
Christine teaches you a way out of shame by helping you rediscover the power of God to overcome our mistakes, our inadequacies, our pasts, our limitations.

**DARE TO DO WHAT
GOD CALL YOU TO**
Learn from Christine life-transforming insights about how to overcome the challenges and often painful circumstances we all experience, and to use those experiences to be a catalyst for change – in ourselves and those around us.

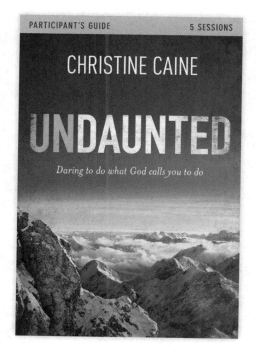

Also Available From Lisa

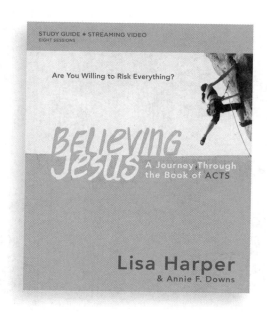

**RISKING EVERYTHING
IS SO WORTH IT**
In this eight-session study,
Lisa reveals how the Holy Spirit
catapults believers forward with
power, grace, and authority to
dramatically impact the world.

PERFECTION NOT REQUIRED
In this eight-session study, Lisa
teaches the gospel that doesn't
celebrate the elite, but embraces
the outliers, outcasts, and
overlooked!

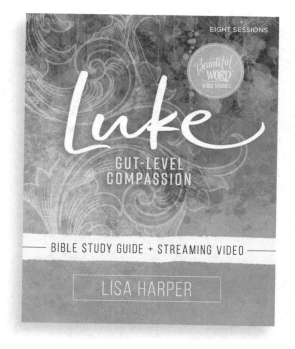

From the Publisher

GREAT STUDIES

ARE EVEN BETTER WHEN THEY'RE SHARED!

Help others find this study:

- Post a review at your favorite online bookseller.

- Post a picture on a social media account and share why you enjoyed it.

- Send a note to a friend who would also love it—or, better yet, go through it with them!

Thanks for helping others grow their faith!

Also From
Lisa and Christine Together

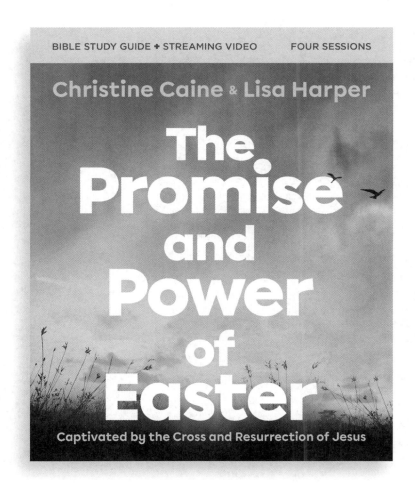

Jesus has commissioned you to come and see for yourself, and then go and tell a lost and broken world that He is alive.